INTEGRITY
OF GOD'S WORD
Study Guide

KENNETH COPELAND

INTEGRITY
OF GOD'S WORD
Study Guide

KENNETH COPELAND

KENNETH COPELAND
PUBLICATIONS

Unless otherwise noted, all scripture is from the *King James Version* of the Bible.

Integrity of God's Word

ISBN-10 1-57562-658-6   30-0718
ISBN-13 978-1-57562-658-1

24 23 22 21 20 19   12 11 10 9 8 7

Kenneth Copeland Publications
Fort Worth, TX 76192-0001

For more information about Kenneth Copeland Ministries, visit kcm.org or call 1-800-600-7395 (U.S. only) or +1-817-852-6000.

1

"Through faith we
understand that the
worlds were framed by
the word of God...."

Hebrews 11:3

God framed the world by His word.
You frame your world the same way.

MESSAGE ONE
Integrity of God's Word–I

God and His Word Are One

*T*he first chapter of Genesis gives us the foundation of how God created the world. "And God said" and His Word carried the power to create what He said.

God Is Bound
by His Word

FOCUS: "Through faith we understand that the worlds were framed by the word of God..." (Hebrews 11:3).

God and His Word are one. He cannot be separated from His Word. His Word has an integrity that is beyond reproach. Just as His nature does not change, neither does His Word. God's Word is His bond and He will not break it.

The world and everything in it was created by the words of God. His faith is released by the words He speaks. Hebrews 11:3 says, "Through faith we understand that the worlds were framed by the word of God." Everything we see in the natural came into existence by the faith-filled words of God. He knew how to put spiritual law into operation and the force of faith to bring into existence all things abiding in Him.

> *Just as God's nature does not change, neither does His Word.*

The same force resides in the born-again believer. It has the ability to respond today just as it did in the beginning. It is called the shield of faith that quenches all the fiery darts of the devil (Ephesians 6:16).

Words Are Power Containers

FOCUS: Jesus said, "For by thy words thou shalt be justified, and by thy words thou shalt be condemned" (Matthew 12:37).

Words are containers. They carry power.

Adam had total authority to rule as god over every living creature on earth. He was to rule by speaking words.

When Adam sinned, he gave his authority over to Satan. God needed an under ruler to perform His Word in the earth. He made a covenant with Abraham. This covenant gave God legal entry into the earth. It was to Abraham and his seed as well as the seed after him. God continued to release His Word through His covenant and Jesus came into the earth.

God releases His faith with His words.

God releases His faith with His words. The words He speaks are alive and full of power. They are active today because they are eternal, settled in heaven forever (Psalm 119:89).

The Word was given to the prophets to make the people free. It was given to Moses to release Israel from bondage. Then it was given to Jesus to make mankind free. John 8:32 says, "And ye shall know the truth, and the truth shall make you free."

God's Word has absolute integrity.
You can be sure of it.
God released His faith through
His Word and you release your
faith in the same way—by speaking
God's Word. Your words are
powerful containers. Today, you
can choose to speak God's Word
and change your world.

Now Begin Enjoying It

The Holy Spirit will perform the faith-filled words that are spoken from the mouth of the believer. The words must be according to God's Word. Proverbs 3:5 says, "Trust in the Lord with all thine heart; and lean not unto thine own understanding." We can trust God because He is eternally true. The words we speak will produce just as if God spoke them Himself because His Word has integrity.

Message 1 Outlined

I. God cannot be separated from His Word
    A. God is one with His Word
    B. His Word is His bond

II. Everything was created by God's Word
    A. He releases faith with His words
    B. Hebrews 11:3

III. The believer has the same ability through the words of his mouth

IV. Words are containers
    A. Matthew 12:37
        1. Justify
        2. Condemn
    B. Words carry spiritual power
        1. Activate God's forces
        2. Activate Satan's forces

V. Jesus is the Word manifested—John 1:14

Study Questions

(1) Why can't God and His Word be separated?

_____

_____

_____

_____

(2) Explain how everything in the physical came into existence.

_____

_____

_____

_____

(3) How did God's Word get back into the earth?

_____

_____

_____

_____

(4) What happened when Adam sinned?

_____

_____

_____

(5) How does God's Word represent His integrity?

_____

_____

_____

Study Notes

"For ever, O Lord, thy word is settled in heaven."
Psalm 119:89

2

"*Sanctify them through thy truth: thy word is truth.*"

John 17:17

To *sanctify* means "to separate" or "set apart."

Are you separated from old habits?

Are you set apart unto the life of God?

MESSAGE TWO

Integrity of God's Word—II

Let the Life in the Word Bring Abundance to Your Life

$\mathcal{G}$od operates by His words.

God Spoke and God Created...
You Speak and You Create

FOCUS: "And God said, Let there be light: and there was light" (Genesis 1:3).

In Genesis 1:2 the Spirit of God was moving over the face of the waters. No creative power was released until God spoke. Faith-filled words released the substance which the Spirit of God used to cause the universe to come into existence. God applied His faith in His words. "And God said, Let there be light: and there was light" (Genesis 1:3). God spoke the words and the Holy Spirit took those words and created a universe.

> *The Word is miraculous in nature when released because of its integrity.*

Faith must be applied to the mountain in order for it to move (Mark 11:23). By understanding how God applies His faith, the believer will know how to apply his faith. Faith is believing and acting on what God has already said. Every word released by God is filled with the force of faith.

At the time of Creation God set into motion a law—the law of Genesis or the law of Beginnings. According to this law, every living thing was created by God to produce after its own kind. When the law is put into motion, it produces after its own kind. The principle is: Whatever is planted is what will be reaped.

Man is a spirit, he has a soul and he lives in a body. The law of Genesis would say: Physical man's life is sustained by physical food which produces natural strength. The mind eats mental food which produces willpower. The spirit of man eats spiritual food which produces faith.

Words of Life for
Your Life of Words

FOCUS: Jesus said, "...the words that I speak unto you, they are spirit, and they are life" (John 6:63).

There is life in the Word of God. Deuteronomy 30:19 says, "...I have set before you life and death, blessing and cursing: therefore choose life." There is absolute life in the Word of God. It comes alive when it is meditated upon. When the be-liever operates this way, death is overtaken by life, sickness is overtaken by healing, poverty is overtaken by prosperity.

> *faith is believing and acting on what God has already said.*

John 17:17 says, "Sanctify them through thy truth: thy word is truth." To *sanctify* means "to separate" or "set apart." Hebrews 4:12 says it is able to *divide* asunder spirit and soul, joints and marrow. God's Word is able to separate the be-liever from Satan's dominion. It will separate those who give their attention to it. The Word is God's system. It contains the principles for living the abundant life in every area.

*Choose life today. Choose the Word
of God today. The Word is sure.
You can stake your life on it!*

Now Begin Enjoying It

Jesus is the Living Word. When you accept Him as Lord, He separates you from the kingdom of Satan. The Word not only separates you from old habits, but from unnecessary things that hinder you from walking successfully in the light of His Word. The Word is miraculous in nature when released because of its integrity. It will not return void!

Message 2 *Outlined*

I.   Faith-filled words are creative words

II. The Word is life
     A. John 6:63
     B. Deuteronomy 30:19

III. The Word sanctifies or separates
     A. Hebrews 4:12
     B. Separation from Satan

IV. Jesus is the Living Word

Study Questions

(1) When and how is the creative power of God released?

_____

_____

_____

(2) Explain the law of Genesis.

_____

_____

_____

_____

(3) When does the Word come alive?

_____

_____

_____

_____

(4) What does the Word separate you from?

_____

_____

_____

_____

(5) How does the Word separate?

_____

_____

_____

_____

Study Notes

"Through faith we understand that the worlds were framed by the word of God, so that things which are seen were not made of things which do appear."

Hebrews 11:3

3

"...If ye continue in my word, then are ye my disciples indeed; And ye shall know the truth, and the truth shall make you free."

John 8:31-32

Put the Word of God first place in your life.

Allow it to be the final authority. Then be

a doer of the Word. You'll experience

freedom in Christ as never before.

MESSAGE THREE

Integrity of God's Word—III

The "New You" Can Do the Same Things That Jesus Did

"*B*eing born again, not of corruptible seed, but of incorruptible, by the word of God, which liveth and abideth for ever."

1 Peter 1:23

Live the Victory by Living the Word

FOCUS: "Therefore if any man be in Christ, he is a new creature: old things are passed away; behold, all things are become new" (2 Corinthians 5:17).

The believer has been born again by the Word of God. It is His creative power through the Word that brings into existence a new species of being at the time of the new birth. The Word is an incorruptible seed that lives forever.

The new creation in Christ is capable of anything when the Word is active in his life. In John 17:15, Jesus said, "I pray not that thou shouldest take them out of the world, but that thou shouldest keep them from the evil." He was praying for His followers to be able to live in the world and yet not be affected by its evil. Jesus lived in the earth and He lived above the evil influences. In verse 18, He said, "As thou hast sent me into the world, even so have I also sent them into the world." The believer is to do the same things as Jesus. As God sent Him, He sent the believer. The same weapons God gave Jesus to carry out the responsibility, He has given to His new creations, the Church. God is a just God and He would not have given this responsibility without power to pull down strongholds.

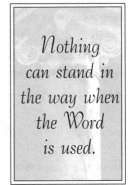

Nothing can stand in the way when the Word is used.

Nothing can stand in the way when the Word is used. Jesus was raised from the pit of hell because of the integrity of God's Word. The Word is powerful and has the ability to deliver man from any bondage of Satan.

The key is the quality decision to put the Word first place and allow it to be final authority. It is not trying the Word, it is being a doer of it. There must be a decision made that God is the source of supply.

Holy Spirit Knowledge Will Create, Invent and Produce

FOCUS: "...That ye might be filled with the knowledge of his will in all wisdom and spiritual understanding" (Colossians 1:9).

In John 8:31 and 32 Jesus said, "If ye continue in my word, then are ye my disciples indeed; And ye shall know the truth, and the truth shall make you free." As the counsel of God is walked in, through the Word, the truth is revealed. The understanding is enlightened to know the snares Satan sets. God will cause the Word to rise up from within to bring freedom and separation from evil.

The Word will separate unnecessary things that try to come between you and your fellowship with God. This is revealed knowledge; not the knowledge that comes from the five physical senses. Sense knowledge will not reveal God or the Word. Hebrews 11:6 says, "But without faith it is impossible to please him: for he that cometh to God must believe that he is, and that he is a rewarder of them that diligently seek him." This is believing regardless of feelings.

> *Exact knowledge is imparted to the spirit of a man by the Spirit of God.*

In Colossians 1:9 Paul prayed "...that ye might be filled with the knowledge of his will in all wisdom and spiritual understanding." The Greek text says "exact knowledge." Exact knowledge is imparted to the spirit of a man by the Spirit of God. It is called revelation knowledge. It is creative and powerful. It is the light of God's Word revealed to the heart of man.

Invest time in the Word, listen to the Holy Spirit and expect to receive the exact knowledge you need.

Now Begin Enjoying It

You have the ability to hear the voice of God as you meditate in the Word and fellowship with God in prayer. This fellowship with the Father causes all things to lose their hold because you have taken time to allow the Word to work in you.

Message 3 Outlined

I.   The Word of God lives and abides forever

II. Believers can walk above evil and not beneath
    A.   John 17:15
    B.   Walk as Jesus walked using the same weapons

III. The Word works in any situation

IV. Decide to put the Word first place
    A.   Be a doer of the Word
    B.   Do not compromise
    C.   John 8:31-32

V.   Allow the Holy Spirit to speak to you
    A.   Sense knowledge will fail
        1.   Comes from five physical senses
        2.   Based on feelings
    B.   Revelation knowledge always triumphs
        1.   Based on the Word
            a.   Faith not feelings
            b.   Hebrews 11:6
        2.   Exact knowledge is from the Holy Spirit
            (Colossians 1:9)
            a.   a. Full knowledge
            b.   Full measure
                i.   Invents
                ii.   Creates
                iii. Produces

Study Questions

(1) How does the believer keep from being under the dominion of evil?

_____

_____

_____

_____

(2) Why is it important to make a quality decision to put God's Word first place?

_____

_____

_____

_____

(3) Why was Jesus given the Spirit of God without measure?

_____

_____

_____

_____

(4) Explain what sense knowledge is.

_____

_____

_____

(5) Explain what revelation knowledge is.

_____

_____

_____

Study Notes

"*That ye might walk worthy of the Lord, unto all pleasing, being fruitful in every good work, and increasing in the knowledge of God.*"
Colossians 1:10

4

"...For I will hasten my word to perform it."

Jeremiah 1:12

Miracles happen
when you speak faith-filled words.

MESSAGE FOUR

The Miracle Action of the Word—I

Your Miracle Is Just a Word Away

God's Word is a living thing. When it is acted on in faith, miracles take place.

God's Part of a Miracle

FOCUS: "So shall my word be that goeth forth out of my mouth: it shall not return unto me void, but it shall accomplish that which I please, and it shall prosper in the thing whereto I sent it" (Isaiah 55:11).

God did not leave His people without His ways and without His thoughts. Even though His thoughts and ways are much higher, they are not out of reach. God sent His Word into the earth. It is likened to the rain and snow that falls to the ground for the purpose of bearing fruit. The Word will not return void and will prosper (bear fruit) where it is sent (Isaiah 55:8-11).

When Moses died, God told Joshua to meditate the Word day and night so he would prosper and succeed (Joshua 1:8). The Word is a living thing. When it is acted upon, the miracle action power of God is released. John 3:21 says, "But he that doeth truth cometh to the light, that his deeds may be made manifest, that they are wrought in God."

> *You're not responsible for performing the Word but to walk in the light of it in faith.*

The believer is not responsible for performing the Word but to walk in the light of it in faith. God said in Jeremiah 1:12, "...For I will hasten my word to perform it." The Word is as valid as a written, signed and notarized will. The difference is that Jesus not only died to make the will of God valid but He rose from the dead to see to it that it is carried out.

Your Part of a Miracle

FOCUS: "…What things soever ye desire, when ye pray, believe that ye receive them, and ye shall have them" (Mark 11:24).

In Matthew 14, Peter asked Jesus to bid him to come to Him. Jesus spoke the word "come" signifying His approval. Peter began to walk to Jesus. When he began to sink, he cried out. He began to look at things around him instead of keeping his eyes on Jesus, the Living Word. God will not go against a man's will, He will not force His miracle power on anyone. Peter allowed doubt to enter into his consciousness.

> *Act on the Word as if it has your name personally written in it.*

Second Corinthians 10:5 says to bring every thought captive to the obedience of Christ. The Word is where the performance is. The believer is to receive the Word and act upon it just as quickly as he would act upon the word of a trusted lawyer or doctor. Act on the Word as if it has your name personally written in it.

The miracle action is released with words. God released His faith with His words. It is the incorruptible seed, which is the Word, that causes the new birth. The seed of the new birth is the miracle-working power of God. When that seed is planted in the inner man, the faith of God is imparted to the spirit and causes a new birth. Second Corinthians 5:17 says, "Therefore if any man be in Christ, he is a new creature: old things are passed away; behold, all things are become new." The new creature can fill his own words with faith and release them with the same authority that God has over His own words. This is because he has been born again, a child of God, created in God's own image.

> *God hastens His Word to perform it—that's His part. Believing His Word and speaking it in faith with the authority He's given you—that's your part.*
>
> *Your part plus His part equals a miracle!*

Now Begin Enjoying It

Jesus is the believer's voice in heaven and the believer is Jesus' voice on earth. When words are spoken according to the Word, the angels obey, causing the thing desired to come to pass (Psalm 103:20).

Mark 11:24 says, "...What things soever ye desire, when ye pray, believe that ye receive them, and ye shall have them." Release the miracle action of the Word today. Make use of your rights and responsibilities as a child of God.

Message 4 Outlined

I.   Miracle action is released through the Word of God
    A.   The Word will not return void
    B.   The Word bears fruit
    C.   John 3:21

II. God performs the Word
    A.   It is not up to the believer to carry out the Word
    B.   Jeremiah 1:12

III. Keep your eyes fixed on Jesus
    A.   Doubt is a thief
    B.   Second Corinthians 10:5

IV. Release the miracle action through your words

S t u d y   Q u e s t i o n s

(1) Compare the process of rain and snow falling to the ground with the Word spoken from the mouth of the believer.

_____

_____

_____

(2) Why did God tell Joshua to meditate the Word day and night?

_____

_____

_____

(3) How is the Word of God like a valid written will?

_____

_____

_____

(4) Why did Peter begin to sink?

_____

_____

_____

(5) Explain how the miracle action of the Word is released and what takes place.

_____

_____

_____

Study Notes

"*Casting down imaginations, and every high thing that exalteth itself against the knowledge of God, and bringing into captivity every thought to the obedience of Christ.*"

2 Corinthians 10:5

5

"Seeing then that we have a great high priest, that is passed into the heavens, Jesus the Son of God, let us hold fast our profession."

Hebrews 4:14

Fear activates Satan the way faith activates God. But you can drive out doubt and fear. You can think and act like God. And you will receive a miracle when you hold fast to your confession of faith.

MESSAGE FIVE
The Miracle Action of the Word—II

Be Bold—Act Like God—
Get the Results God Gets!

*T*he Word of God is alive. It will prosper where it is sent. It creates life when it is activated in faith.

A Fearful Mind or a Faith-Filled Mind?

FOCUS: "Be ye therefore followers of God, as dear children" (Ephesians 5:1).

God's Word in man will accomplish the same results that rain does in the earth. It will bud and grow on the inside of a man so he is able to do the things that God does.

Ephesians 5:1 says to be followers of God as children are followers of their parents. The Greek word for "followers" is translated into the English word "mimic." The believer is to act like God as a child mimics his parents. In John 14:9 Jesus said, "...He that hath seen me hath seen the Father." God intends for His children to act like Him. Act like God, believe His Word and the signs will follow.

> *Act like God, believe His Word and the signs will follow.*

Think like God thinks. A worried mind is not a mind controlled by the Word. It is not the mind of Christ in operation. It is not energized by faith. A mind that is operating in fear is not operating in faith. The world is controlled by the force of fear. It is the very nature of Satan. When Adam committed high treason he began to operate in fear. Satan became his illegitimate stepfather. Fear activates Satan the way faith activates God.

Pray the Answer

FOCUS: "Be careful for nothing; but in every thing by prayer and supplication with thanksgiving let your requests be made known unto God; and the peace of God, which passeth all understanding, shall keep your hearts and minds through Christ Jesus" (Philippians 4:6-7).

When the Word, prayed in faith, is released in our prayer life, the miracle action of God's Word is released. In Genesis chapter 15, Abraham needed direction from God. He was told to give a sacrifice and when it was consumed he would have the answer. When the birds came to steal the sacrifice, Abraham had to drive them away. God did not keep the birds away. Abraham did.

When the Word is activated in prayer, it is starting with the answer. Jesus prayed the answer in the Lord's Prayer (Matthew 6:9-13). Put the Word up before the Father and read it out loud. Do not seek counsel from others about whether the Word is true. Satan will bring contrary thoughts and circumstances but immediately cast them down with the Word. God's Word will not work unless it is taken and believed as the Spirit of God reveals it to you. Satan's lies will not be effective unless they are received and believed. The believer is the establishing witness.

> *A mind that is operating in fear is not operating in faith.*

Make a quality decision to stand on the Word and stay in peace. Indecision is walking in Satan's territory. After the Word is activated in prayer, watch it go to work. Hebrews 4:14 says to hold fast your profession or confession. You cannot hold fast to your confession of faith if it is not based on the Word.

Say what God says in His Word about your situation. Then hold fast to your confession of faith. Speak the Word only. Results are sure to follow!

Now Begin Enjoying It

Most Christians fail in their prayer life because they don't know the answer to begin with. Jesus is the answer. The Word is the answer.

Do not hesitate to use the Word. He is watching over it to see that it is performed (Isaiah 55:11).

Message 5 Outlined

I.   The Word produces life

II. Act like God as a child acts like his parent
   A.   Think like God
   B.   Operate in faith instead of fear

III. The Word is God's part of our prayer life
   A.   Genesis 15:11—Abraham drove off the birds of prey
   B.   Lay the Word on the altar; watch over it so the birds of prey (Satan and his angels) will not steal it

IV. Make the decision to stand on the Word
   A.   Indecision will not accomplish anything
   B.   Hold fast to your confession (Philippians 4:6-9; 1 Peter 5:6-7)

V.   A successful prayer life begins with finding the answer in the Word

Study Questions

(1) How can the believer do the things that God does?

_____

_____

_____

_____

(2) Why is it important to think as God does?

_____

_____

_____

_____

(3) Explain what it means to put the Word on the altar of prayer.

_____

_____

_____

_____

(4) What is the importance of making a quality decision?

_____

_____

_____

_____

(5) Why do Christians fail in their prayer life?

_____

_____

_____

Study Notes

"So shall my word be that goeth forth out of my mouth: it shall not return unto me void, but it shall accomplish that which I please, and it shall prosper in the thing whereto I sent it."

Isaiah 55:11

6

"And why call ye me, Lord, Lord, and do not the things which I say? Whosoever cometh to me, and heareth my sayings, and doeth them, I will shew you to whom he is like: He is like a man which built an house, and digged deep, and laid the foundation on a rock: and when the flood arose, the stream beat vehemently upon that house, and could not shake it: for it was founded upon a rock."

Luke 6:46-48

The storms of life will come. But there's nothing to fear when your house stands firmly, fearlessly and faithfully on the Word of God.

MESSAGE SIX
Acting on the Word

Feelings, Failure and Fear Bow to Faith…Every Time

God releases His faith with His words. The Word of God is filled with the faith of God. It is His integrity. When the believer activates his faith and receives that Word, God's miracle-working power is released.

Walking in Faith Is
Walking Above the Pressure

FOCUS: "...Upholding all things by the word of his power" (Hebrews 1:3).

Being a man of your word will not do much good until someone receives and acts upon your word. A relationship between two people will not grow if there is no trust in each other's words. There will only be doubt and fear. The same thing is true with God. His integrity is His Word. It must be believed and then activated in faith.

The integrity of the Word means nothing until it is used. Always consider the Word. When pressure comes, go to the Word instead of the natural. The things done in the natural will only cause the pressure to be temporarily subdued or forgotten. By using the Word, the pressure will be done away with. God's Word will cause you to walk above pressure.

Walk by faith and not by sight, even when it appears in all natural circumstances to be a futile situation. Failure comes from not knowing how to apply and stand in the protection of the Word. It is important to know how to use the shield of faith in order to stop the wiles of the devil.

Jesus said to continue in the Word. You will know the truth and the truth will make you free (John 8:31, 32). If not, the pressure will become great, resulting in failure to resist. Mark, the fourth chapter, talks about those who hear the Word with gladness and receive it. Then when persecution

> *Failure comes from not knowing how to apply and stand in the protection of the Word.*

and affliction come for the Word's sake they are offended because they have no root in themselves. They did not take time to meditate the Word. So when pressure came, instead of standing firm, they fell.

Now Is the Time to Act on the Word

FOCUS: "…The just shall live by faith" (Galatians 3:11).

Jesus said that the man who hears His words and does them is one who has built his house on a solid foundation. When the floods arise, the man is prepared and cannot be shaken because he is founded on a rock. The time to act on the Word is not after the flood has hit. The time to act on the Word is now (Luke 6:46-49).

Galatians 3:11 says, "…The just shall live by faith." Do not wait to use faith after sickness, disease and poverty strike. Begin now by meditating the Word so you will be strong in the Lord. The attacks will still come from Satan but you will be strong. You will be victorious over his attacks. God would rather His children develop and mature in His Word while everything is going well rather than when the pressure hits.

By staying in fellowship with the Father you will be sensitive to the leading of the Holy Spirit. Jesus said that the Spirit of Truth will guide you into all truth (John 16:13). You will know when Satan is going to come against you and you will be ready for it. You can take control of those things in the spirit before they ever get to you.

*When your foundation is solid,
built on the Word of God, no storm
of life will be able to destroy you.*

Now Begin Enjoying It

John 15:7 says, "If ye abide in me, and my words abide in you, ye shall ask what ye will, and it shall be done unto you." This is not just a once in a while thing, it is a living communion. Keep the Word before you and take your mind off of what you feel, think and see. Then when the flood comes, your house will be solid and nothing will destroy it because you have made a quality decision to stand on God's Word.

Message 6 *Outlined*

I.   Integrity is worthless unless it is received and acted upon

II. Consider the Word
   A.   Hebrews 1:3, all things are upheld by the Word of His power
   B.   Do not consider the natural
   C.   Walk above pressure
   D.   Walk by faith, not by sight
   E.   Failure comes from lack of the Word
   F.   John 8:31-32—the truth will make you free

III. Be a doer of the Word
   A.   Build on the solid rock
   B.   Act on the Word before the flood hits
      1.   Galatians 3:11
      2.   Use faith now

IV. Fellowship with the Father
   A.   John 16:3
   B.   John 15:7

Study Questions

(1) Explain the importance of acting on integrity.

_____

_____

_____

_____

(2) In a pressure situation why is it necessary to go to the Word?

_____

_____

_____

_____

(3) What causes failure and how is it prevented?

_____

_____

_____

(4) What happens to the believer who builds his house on the rock?

_____

_____

_____

_____

(5) Why is it important to be sensitive to the Holy Spirit?

_____

_____

_____

_____

Study Notes

"But be ye doers of the word, and not hearers only,
deceiving your own selves."
James 1:22

Prayer for Salvation and Baptism in the Holy Spirit

Heavenly Father, I come to You in the Name of Jesus. Your Word says, "Whosoever shall call on the name of the Lord shall be saved" (Acts 2:21). I am calling on You. I pray and ask Jesus to come into my heart and be Lord over my life according to Romans 10:9-10: "If thou shalt confess with thy mouth the Lord Jesus, and shalt believe in thine heart that God hath raised him from the dead, thou shalt be saved. For with the heart man believeth unto righteousness; and with the mouth confession is made unto salvation." I do that now. I confess that Jesus is Lord, and I believe in my heart that God raised Him from the dead. I repent of sin. I renounce it. I renounce the devil and everything he stands for. Jesus is my Lord.

I am now reborn! I am a Christian—a child of Almighty God! I am saved! You also said in Your Word, "If ye then, being evil, know how to give good gifts unto your children: HOW MUCH MORE shall your heavenly Father give the Holy Spirit to them that ask him?" (Luke 11:13). I'm also asking You to fill me with the Holy Spirit. Holy Spirit, rise up within me as I praise God. I fully expect to speak with other tongues as You give me the utterance (Acts 2:4). In Jesus' Name. Amen!

Begin to praise God for filling you with the Holy Spirit. Speak those words and syllables you receive—not in your own language, but the language given to you by the Holy Spirit. You have to use your own voice. God will not force you to speak. Don't be concerned with how it sounds. It is a heavenly language!

Continue with the blessing God has given you and pray in the spirit every day.

You are a born-again, Spirit-filled believer. You'll never be the same! Find a good church that boldly preaches God's Word and obeys it. Become part of a church family who will love and care for you as you love and care for them.

We need to be connected to each other. It increases our strength in God. It's God's plan for us.

Make it a habit to watch the Believer's Voice of Victory Network and become a doer of the Word, who is blessed in his doing (James 1:22-25).

About the Author

Kenneth Copeland is co-founder and president of Kenneth Copeland Ministries in Fort Worth, Texas, and best-selling author of books that include *Honor—Walking in Honesty, Truth and Integrity,* and *THE BLESSING of The LORD Makes Rich and He Adds No Sorrow With It.*

Since 1967, Kenneth has been a minister of the gospel of Christ and teacher of God's Word. He is also the artist on award-winning albums such as his Grammy-nominated *Only the Redeemed, In His Presence, He Is Jehovah, Just a Closer Walk* and *Big Band Gospel.* He also co-stars as the character Wichita Slim in the children's adventure videos *The Gunslinger, Covenant Rider* and the movie *The Treasure of Eagle Mountain,* and as Daniel Lyon in the Commander Kellie and the Superkids™ videos *Armor of Light* and *Judgment: The Trial of Commander Kellie.* Kenneth also co-stars as a Hispanic godfather in the 2009 and 2016 movies *The Rally* and *The Rally 2: Breaking the Curse.*

With the help of offices and staff in the United States, Canada, England, Australia, South Africa and Ukraine, Kenneth is fulfilling his vision to boldly preach the uncompromised WORD of God from the top of this world, to the bottom, and all the way around. His ministry reaches millions of people worldwide through daily and Sunday TV broadcasts, magazines, teaching audios and videos, conventions and campaigns, and the World Wide Web.

Learn more about Kenneth Copeland Ministries
by visiting our website at **kcm.org**

Believer's Voice of **VICTORY**

When The LORD first spoke to Kenneth and Gloria Copeland about starting the *Believer's Voice of Victory* magazine...

He said: *This is your seed. Give it to everyone who ever responds to your ministry, and don't ever allow anyone to pay for a subscription!*

For more than 50 years, it has been the joy of Kenneth Copeland Ministries to bring the good news to believers. Readers enjoy teaching from ministers who write from lives of living contact with God, and testimonies from believers experiencing victory through God's WORD in their everyday lives.

Today, the *BVOV* magazine is mailed monthly, bringing encouragement and blessing to believers around the world. Many even use it as a ministry tool, passing it on to others who desire to know Jesus and grow in their faith!

Request your FREE subscription to the *Believer's Voice of Victory* magazine today!

Go to **freevictory.com** to subscribe online, or call us at **1-800-600-7395** (U.S. only) or **+1-817-852-6000**.

We're Here for You!®

Your growth in God's WORD and victory in Jesus are at the very center of our hearts. In every way God has equipped us, we will help you deal with the issues facing you, so you can be the **victorious overcomer** He has planned for you to be.

The mission of Kenneth Copeland Ministries is about all of us growing and going together. Our prayer is that you will take full advantage of all The LORD has given us to share with you.

Wherever you are in the world, you can watch the *Believer's Voice of Victory* broadcast on television (check your local listings), the Internet at kcm.org or on our digital Roku channel.

Our website, **kcm.org,** gives you access to every resource we've developed for your victory. And, you can find contact information for our international offices in Africa, Australia, Canada, Europe, Ukraine and our headquarters in the United States.

Each office is staffed with devoted men and women, ready to serve and pray with you. You can contact the worldwide office nearest you for assistance, and you can call us for prayer at our U.S. number, 1-817-852-6000, seven days a week!

We encourage you to connect with us often and let us be part of your everyday walk of faith!

Jesus Is LORD!

Kenneth & Gloria Copeland

Kenneth and Gloria Copeland